Love through her I's

A book of poetry authored by:
Iesha S. Williams

Book cover illustration by:
DeMarus Rogers

Illustrations by:
Monrovia Ndaiye

MCNAE, MARLIN & MACKENƷIE, LTD.
PUBLISHERS, BY SPECIAL APPOINTMENT
GLASGOW • NEW YORK • LOS ANGELES
QUEENS ROAD, GLASGOW, LANARKSHIRE G42 800 SCOTLAND

Dedications:

To my amazing sister **Maya**; I Love you and I believe in you. May your words ignite the souls of many, as well as provide you healing for your own pain. Put God first and never stop writing.

To my husband **Mark**; for being proof that God hears my prayers, who completely believes in me, inspires me and Loves me to no end

To **Ma** and **Pa**; for your unchanging and unwavering Love; it saved my life

Grandpa: for the example of your unwavering Faith in God and unmovable Love for **Grandma**

Mommy: for fighting through your pain enough to Love and trust again, for apologizing and for pursuing who God is calling you to be. Your strength and resilience inspire me.

Dad: For choosing to Love me

To all those in pain, who see no end, in search of Freedom and Peace; it all starts with you. Love yourselves enough to see past your pain. And yes, you deserve Love, believe it.

Foreword: With Love, anything is possible and with God even more is possible. I am so thankful to God for His unwavering Grace and Mercy. I am thankful to God for His undying and unconditional Love. I am thankful for the truth and I encourage you all who are reading this; to find it for yourself. It won't look like everyone else's, so don't aspire to anyone or anything but what God has designed for you; and this comes with DILIGENTLY and FAITHFULLY seeking Him. Working for a relationship that will be like no other and using your pain as a testimony to encourage and uplift others. There is healing in acknowledgment of your pain and flaw; God honors and Loves us for this. There are many blessings on the other side of what you are facing, so don't EVER give up. In the midst, it never seems that way but find Comfort, Joy and Assurance that God is always with you. I am thankful to God for so many chances to get it right.

Everything on this earth is temperamental, conditional, unforgiving and hasty; nothing of substance can grow or be nurtured in this state. And NOTHING on this earth will ever exceed what God will do for you. We lose sight when we lose our sight. We lose hope when things are their darkest and our need to want to control everything often supersedes our need to be humble and fully commit to God. True commitment entails honesty; facing the raw truth about ourselves and within that, lies great discomfort and disbars many of the beliefs we've told ourselves about ourselves. Most of us cling to a false sense of security out of fear because we won't know what to do when it's gone. Having God in your life is not just acknowledging His presence but living your life to constantly honor Him and honoring your highest God self.. Love yourself enough to **find your truth**.

Peace

Prelude: Love is the foundation of Humanity. God resides within us, within our will and is the source of infinite Power and Enlightenment. Positive thinking combined with positive action creates a cycle of goodness to forever be returned back to you. Live in truth; the proclamation of true Love begins with you.

INFLECTIONS OF LOVE

Love... I've always wanted to Love and be Loved but always looked in the darkest and emptiest places to find it. It'd be easy for me to play the victim each and every time, with each and every person that has hurt me because I just wasn't aware of the detriment of my decisions. But I cannot evade the fact that while I was in that state, I hurt others as well. I didn't Love myself and there is danger in looking to fill a void with someone or something else. If how you feel about yourself is contingent upon a person's approval, what do you do when they're gone? Essentially, their Love will NEVER be enough to sustain. It was impossible to seek in others what I didn't myself, embody; because in order to embody I had to first be able to properly identify. There was no way I could ever find the Love I needed, when I didn't Love myself the way that I needed to. I was out to fill a void; I felt unloved and the insecurity is what I dispelled and ultimately attracted.

No matter how much control I thought I had, my decisions were being made out of needing to fulfill the lack I felt. I was prisoner to the seeking of external validation because it gave me a momentary high. We take discomfort within ourselves as defeat and use it to victimize ourselves over and over. Discomfort is indicative of us needing to change something; however it's not always an external change. It becomes a vicious cycle; it begins with momentary gratification and feeling a high, the high doesn't last and we feel hurt/empty again; gravitate to external blame, instead of identifying the common denominator in every equation; which is us.

I then realized, things don't happen TO US, they happen FOR US. Once I stopped looking at myself as a victim, I was able to walk toward resolution and be empowered by the very flaws I embodied. Self Love is imperative to our well being. These select pieces are attributed to my constant battles and conversations with self about Love.

To know God is to Love your whole self...

So Much

So much, too many
Don't know where to start, where's the beginning?
A lot to deal with, yea there's plenty
Can't find the starting point but I can see myself finishing
Maybe I'm jumping the gun because I just want it to be done
Figuring out my life, that is
One day be successful
maybe have a good relationship
Not only with God or the opposite sex, but with myself as well
It's obvious it starts with me and no one else…

So hard to Love someone so imperfect
Yet I have to Love myself for my imperfections
Everyday I look in the mirror
But like everyone else, fail to see past my own reflection
Personal pain and lack of success lead to the heavy burden of my unhappiness
Have I failed like the rest or is this merely a test?
Only the strong survive
I guess I should be thankful to God I'm alive
Because any less of a person couldn't have revived

So much rests on my shoulders and I'm just getting so much older
The days are growing colder and the world goes no slower
So much, too many
Don't know where to start but there's plenty
Where is my beginning? Where is my ending?

Grip

Anger grips my heart; overwhelmingly leading my actions
to wanna do harm
This is not me
Rather; not the me that I've come to accept

See, the problem is
I run from parts of me that I feel are unfinished
But this anger takes away from the best that I can be

Guilt, worry and insecurities take over me
Stifling my wish to be free

What is the cost of freedom?
How do I begin to free myself?
For me, there is no fear of hell
Because I'm already trapped in it
Mental anguish but quick to dismiss the sh*t
Silently holding on
Wishing someone would just grab my hand

Because…
I'm not good at asking for help

Please take it
I don't want to be led anywhere
Just comforted

No Longer

My consciousness weighs heavy
Because there's so much going on
I am no longer emotionally available
Nor do I wanna be strong
Though strength already resonates in me
I can't find it in me to be the girl they always expect me to
be

My reality is having dealt with the trauma by myself
Expected to rise to the given abuse and put my pain on the
shelf

I can't do it
I can't do it
I can't do it

So much anger

I try to live my life right
And Love past my pain that I've spent years suppressing
Thinking if I'm the bigger person that it would be a blessing
All it has gotten me was nothing

I'm forced to refrain
And remain in the realm of expectations that I'm
imprisoned to

Rewind

In the midst of seeking validation
I settle for less
Urgency at its best
Nevertheless
Bottomless Pit

Stench overwhelming because I've learned to wallow in my
own sh*t
Regret the steps I've failed to take
Afraid that Love has made a mistake
Rewind the time to when your heart was still in its right
place

Back in the days
When mommy stayed and daddy's presence didn't leave
me tainted
I remained faithful in my innocent rage

Complacent;
Thinking that Love would be adjacent
to my happiness
But how can I know Love when my version of it is jaded?
Worthless thoughts weakened my soul
Allowing the world to grasp what I've fought so hard to hold
onto

Them too?
No, can't blame anyone but myself,
I sabotage self
Constructive ways devoured by instant decisions
Filling a void because Love has always been missing

Would've Been but Will Be

What would've happened if dad was there?
What would've happened if mom was able to show she cared, just a little more?

What would've happened if the Love that I showed was reciprocated?
What would've happened if I never had to undo mistrust that was paved by my painful past?

What would've happened if there was consistency in place of instability?

What would've happened, if under one roof; there was one family with peace and harmony?

What would've happened if I got my preconceived notion of the nurture I thought I was sure to receive?
Would I then be a better version of me?

Plunging into my heart deeper after I've already removed the sword
I used to dwell in Love from a hopeless place
But I see that God makes no mistakes
So in the meantime I will pray

That I can forgive, to Love entirely

Yesterday

I wish I could forget what yesterday felt like
But I would have to forgive myself to no longer feel that pain

Allowing myself to be used
And the damage that has sustained

Sometimes, it's hard to get through a day without feeling this way
Subconsciously inflicting my insecurities on others
Who would never put me in harms way

But for now I remain in what seems like shambles
Knowing that choosing to Love another without Loving myself
Would be a huge gamble

I walk around trying to be strong like I'm not phased
Hoping that Love could save my failing grace
Hoping that Love can somehow hide my shame

Hoping that Love doesn't push me away because of my excessive need for its validation
The rush soothes my pain

I feel like I've come to some type of elation
An epiphany, if you will

Feeling like an addict
Who's gotten back their will
to live…

I try to embrace the present
Look forward to my tomorrows
Even if I have to borrow
The Faith seems so lost
I have to learn to forgive myself
Or I will have to deal with a great loss

The loss of self

Long for a Love

I've longed for a Love
That surpasses Human expectation
Surpasses my need to be right
Validates me beyond my extremities

A Love that cleanses my soul
Igniting a desire to grow
In happiness and in truth

I've longed for a Love
A Love so big
It covers up my ugly scars

A Love so big, the reading of its story comes in parts
Legendary

I've longed for a Love

A Love I've never been given by my earthly dad
A Love I've often and freely given
To the undeserving
Sought out in others who often deceived me
Love that led my Faith astray
The pain kept me from discovering
What has always been promised to me
Prevented me from forgiving
And kept me imprisoned
Because Loving on this earth often seems to come with a
price
Comes with pain and strife
Comes with disappointment
And sometimes comes with pride

But I know the Love that I've longed for
Has been here all along
While I searched, it already resonated in me
Made me strong
It gave me will on days I wanted my last breath

I am thankful for God's Love

A Love I've longed for
It saved my life.

Made by Love

We were made by Love
We were made in Love
We were made to Love

So Love should be the innate response to all that is
afflicted upon the Human race

We hold our hearts high; yet we are a disgrace

We put the meaning of truth to shame
We are overpowered by convenience
We are overshadowed by inequity

Where is this balance beam that life should present to me?

There is no balance if you are not present in each moment
that life gives

The irony is that we live to expect
When we should expect to give
For that is where the true balance lies

Reciprocity isn't dead; it has died
We all have our hands out; expecting handouts
When Love is the proof of a perfect humanity

Instead, we are taught to hate the very being that is us
So who do we trust?
When our flesh lusts after worldly attire
Garmented in sin
How do we expect Love to win?"

Forever

On the cusp of forever
I repent my sins
Hoping that God sees my heart filled with pure intentions
I fall short of His grace
But His Love still remains
Never swindled or swayed
Though I've gone astray

My ego has kept me caught up in establishing things on
my time
And in my own ways
But relinquishing control has kept me safe from
My immediately gratifying ways

Sacrifice and time keep me in His Grace because acting in
haste does not save

On the cusp of forever
My knees bent, I pray
That even in my imperfection
He reserves a place

In Love with Love

Love can seem contradicting
Evicting my soul from my reality
Reciprocity seems to be my payment
But I'm paying for the back rent of past tenants
Never allowing me to see
Shades over your windows
Peephole to your soul
You let me peek, even open the door
But never allowing me to enter
Never allowing me to experience
How much more rent do I have to pay?
I'm a new tenant
Give me a chance and let me prove I can
Maintain this place to stay
Allow us to build and get that old furniture out of here
It has so much wear and tear
No one can even sit down in here

A wall for security
Parameters around your actions
Scared to show me how much you want me
Boxed out of intentions
Sights of losing touch
If you only realized how I Love you so much

More or Less

The idea of me sounds good
But do you have what it takes?
To be consistent with your Love instead of taking me for
granted and Loving me in vain
Does Loving me ease the pain that remains from your last?
Can you see me in your future or am I just better than your
past?
Convenience is not a display of your authenticity
Love is simplicity
So let go and receive the best of me

My desire and passion seep from my pores
Leaving you overwhelmed; savoring every drop
Not knowing how much more I have in store
No assembly required
Do not treat me like those of your past mistakes
When the mere expression of "their" Love to you never
correlated with what they say
I want you to stay
But I am perplexed
I cannot stay if you continue to treat me less

What's to Fear?

What separates me from the rest?
Do not detest my acquisition
For it puts me in a position
to grow
To know my strengths and admittedly get to know the destiny God holds
That each layer of adversity unfolds

I am stronger than my greatest fear, though I lay in the belly of it
My passion surges to the top
Forcing me not to quit
To take control of it
So I will
Better yet…
I do
What is the worst to fear?
People mock and hate what they cannot control and understand
What I need to do is let go of fear and embrace confidence in God's plan

Opposition

Faced with opposition
In constant search of resolution

Amidst confusion
I try to stay rooted

But I may be fooled
And find my ways engulfed in shallow intentions
Momentary gain
Human variation of societal corrode
Flesh infested actions
Wondering why I can't reach the greatness desired

Self Affirmations

I walk into the day with my head held high; above momentary satisfaction

All I want to draw to me is the positivity and Love that I seek
Changing my reality starts with a change in me
Taking accountability for being human and my core beliefs
Instilling Faith in my confusion
So that the planned greatness attained is more than an illusion
I vow to me, to be what it is I fervently seek.

She's Kept

She keeps Love in her heart
She's had such a rough start
And her pain seemingly has no ending
Though the life she's living breathes Love into many
Unintentional but purposeful
Natural and informal
Her beauty lies in the purity of her intentions
She bears the hurt from a generational curse
As a result, she splurges on societal pollution
Choking on her demise
Instead of working toward resolution
Her mind struggles to find balance between right and sanity
She looks in the mirror but sees no reflection of her vanity
Blasphemy
She's been exposed to the wicked
But delves in the light of truth

I Digress

Taste the sweet poison that leaves you paralyzed
The one that stifles all of your senses
And floods your intuition with pride
Strokes your egocentric values
While you invest your time believing in pretty lies
Egotistical values, leaving you to rely on self
Demoralization for instant gratification
Is this regime part of your truth?
Making excuses for everything you do
And everything you lack
No accountability depicted on your moral map
It's so much easier to blame
A routine so insane
With expectation of success
A sense of entitlement
Feeling we deserve better without doing
Living for others
Living to impress your peers with a style of dress
Pointing at others while your life is a mess
I digress
From this societal mess
Reckless; endangerment to the soul
The need to always be in control
Our will to chase the tangible is so relentless
We're all so diluted from truth
Are you the problem or are you the solution?

I Am

Never again to live in the repressed version of me
Never again, will I put a "you" before me
"You" can no longer claim my victory
I proclaim strength, faith, and dignity
I once focused on the Love I can give to others
but realize that I have to give this to myself
Inspired to be
Beyond the confines of my insecurities
Beyond the confines of the idealized societal realm of
beauty

Fear no longer holds my heart captive
And past pain does not leave me stagnated, suppressed
and blind

I am
Greater than the victimization I've used as my stance.

I am.

Illusion

I detect that I am much more than a reflection
I protest any critique I subject myself to due to society's obsession
With perfection
A concept flawed because we are all in life's law
Human
So let me erase this perplexity
This confusion

It is all an illusion
Alluding you to insecurity
Society teaches us to strive in an effort to survive
As if the gift of life
Is not worth living
To satisfy our egos, we engage in momentary validation to soothe the discomfort of an unmade face

We all strive to be good enough, searching for external measures

But we have already been equipped with all necessary treasures
We just have to dig deep to find
Shut out the outside
It can be corrupt and vile for your soul
Purge ego and pride
Let go and be human
It is the right to BE FREE in your mind
Of the cognitive dissonance that plagues our hope, faith and abilities

The Dark Side

In the depths of me
I struggle with reasoning for doing what I do
Doing anything out of supposed reasoning does not suffice
Because on good merit alone, I can barely survive
I'm ready to take this mask off
Evade my soul of the responsibility of caring and consequence
What will "they" think of me then; when I expose the dark that only I can see?

Truth & Light

Her words are the light to the pathway she walks on
Her actions effortlessly embody all that she speaks
She magnified and glorified God even as she wept
The delivery of her message came at any expense

The price she was willing to pay to pave the way for the
generations of women
Her proceeds would be more than she could ever profit
monetarily
Walking in grace but ready to fight
Never letting a man determine her worth
God made her in Love and that is what she so deserves
Keep walking even when you don't know your way
Be all that you are and get rid of what you think you aren't
or can't do
You cannot prove what you have not attempted to do
Do not live in fear
For there is always a new beginning when the "end" is near

DEFLECTIONS OF LOVE

If only you knew, how much I could've Loved you… I Love hard and I used to make all sorts of apologies for it. I Loved others more than I Loved myself and for that I would fall. I would often sacrifice my well being for their comfort; subjected myself to abuse and accepted much less than I deserved. Treated inhumanely at the hands of my captors but still feeling sympathy and empathy for them; slight case of Stockholm Syndrome, maybe? I wanted someone who valued me enough to save me, to validate me with their Love because I never saw myself as enough.

Through painful experiences, I found that the only person that could save me, was me. There was nothing wrong with Loving hard and that wasn't the reason for me constantly getting hurt. I have no regrets because it is through Love that I discovered myself and my worth. The pain from the experiences forced me to look at the common factor; which was me and for that I had to evolve if I wanted change. I am thankful that God provided me with the ability to Love despite the void I repeatedly attempted to fill with conditional human temperament and lust. I am thankful for the light at the end of the tunnel. There was an end to pain and I worked toward it before I knew it to be true.

...and when she Loves

Stay

Sweet songs and melodies we make
Because I know in my chaotic heart that despite it all
You want to stay
Confusions is the mask you wear on your face
But my unstable mind makes no mistakes
Because we relate
We remain in the universe's grasp,
Outer-space
Heaven Bound
Our connection sound
as the horns blare from Heaven's gates
Endless possibilities as vast as your "see"
A contradiction is what you see
Beautiful is what I consider us to be

Remains, Remain

In we I trust
In our connection I lust
I will pay attention if you promise to do the same
I will fight for us if you promise to remain
True
In us, to me, to you
Follow the depths of your heart to ignite our fire
Our deepest desires, unspoken of
But felt
like the Faith from God above
Let's conquer this life
You know I'll fight
I want us to be right
Before one of us gets left
So let's move forward
Start a new book; never a new chapter
Realistic, no fairytale
Happily every after
Here's to our beautiful disaster

No Other Way

I know no other way to give than to give all that I can
I believed in the potential of him and what we could be
Not the reality of what was
But I am proud that through it all
I Love, have Loved and will continue to Love despite his inability to Love me past the sole benefits of himself

Remnants of Love stained my truth of him, overpowering the stench of his disregard and irreverence for anything other than himself

But I will not be stifled by empty promises nor will I victimize myself with what ifs

If only he believed in me like I did in him
But it's ok, I'm ok. I forgive you.

Specific Anonymity

You get the gist of me
While others speculate based on their worldly values

Their perception is tainted by an ever changing society
Instantly gratifying their insecurities
And frequently over simplifying
Due to their ability…

Well….

Inability to relate

But I Love who you are to me
You could rob the whole world blind
While screaming you Love me
I believe it
I believe you
I believe in our fate
Though fear burdens my intellect
I know better than to equate it
To the lack of Love I've always been shown

Better than the rest
Safe to say; you're the best
Only because our Love is our own
Love me today, like tomorrow will never come
And when tomorrow comes Love me until I'm done

For you, I will shed pride and indulge in vulnerability
Because I know you will keep my heart safe

Counterfeit

I thought he was IT
Until he turned out to be counterfeit
Using my Love as an expenditure
Gave him plenty but he kept taking more

More, but I couldn't afford the price he had me paying

Emotions I displayed
but he put my Love to shame
Used after the hurt he knew I endured
Basking on a journey
In which I thought our Love was pure

But he lured me with his seemingly humble grace and
poetic ways

He played me just like the string on his guitar
Now, I'm here wondering how it got this far

Anyone that gets close, you push them away with your
leech like ways

You are more comfortable with those who feed this image
you sell yourself to be

People that don't know the real you
So you have no accountability
Because they vibe off of what they see

When you perform; claiming to be a man
But where was your manhood when my Love paid all your
bills

Blinded by charm and your potential
Telling me you Love me was just a sham
Couldn't believe you treated me this way; I'm still trying to
understand
You lack manhood
This visage you claim

At this point, I just pray to forget your name.

Can't Pretend

In desperation for physical elation, I open my arms to you
My need for validation through conversation fed my belief
in you

But you were not worthy of my Love

I can't pretend that it doesn't hurt me
I can't pretend that what you've done doesn't affect me
But the best thing you've done is desert me

Allowing me to really experience the man you really were
Not that your words could concur

Nothing is a blur
Things have been so clear
I let me needing to be Loved instill a level of fear

But no worries my dear, your lack of accountability has
shown me my strength
I can do better by myself
And
I don't need your mess

Do You Still?

Do you still think of me?
Do I succeed your need to be?

So much time has passed since I've felt your kiss and
heard the joy that my presence used to bring
Instead, I sit in your absence and divulge in the loneliness
you have left for me

I'm still wondering after all I've given you, if loneliness and
deceit was the only gift you were capable of giving
Now I'm left with the memory of never
Trapped in our yesterdays' of Love.

I Ain't Change

I'm quite content in simplicity
My peace is way more valuable to me than "popularity"
Not every spectator clicks "like"
Not everyone who calls themselves your friend has your best interest in mind

Some just want an in to your personal business and never want to see you doing "better than them"

They will watch you scramble to your feet after being on your hands and knees
Will not help you but wanna celebrate with you
I will always be respectful and courteous, that's just me
Because

I am who I am first
Your insecurity and negative ways will never change me

But don't expect my loyalty because when I was starving; you weren't tryna help feed me

Now I'm feastin' and for sure you're around

All in my space but when I was low you were nowhere to be found

Those are the same "friends" talking about you changed…
No, I just saw your ways and quickly decided to switch lanes

Delight

I bask in the delight of your smile
Embark on the uniqueness of your style
Worthwhile
It's been a long time since I've experienced this
This….

This?
Whatever it is
A verbal description couldn't depict it

But I reminisce

On the Love we had
Because it feels as though I met you forever ago

It feels as though I've met my match
Flame ignited
Spark it up
Until I make you high

So abrupt
You freely disrupt my desire to mistrust
I lust
For your heart

A need for us to prevail as a single entity
Enter me

Fill me up
Overflow

Perfectly imperfect

No amount of time can define
So inspired by this chance
So, shall we dance?

Can I Have You?

Just know that
My walls are built up so high
But I want you to tear them down
Not in destruction
But still serving as my dynamite
And
Making me explode

As my King
Wear this crown
I extend my Love and loyalty
And in passion, I am bound
Bound to you by fearlessness
Allow me in the depths of your mentality
Have faith in me through the depths of your spirituality
There is no coincidence in the crossing of our paths
So do not deny me the need to feed you the lack

Undo

In all my sincerity, allow me to pour my heart into you
So much conspiring in the world
But the pain from your past
My Love can undo

So let me Love you
Be open enough to reciprocate
Allow my intensity to integrate
Your segregated ways
Because you know…
Not all women are the same
I understand the pain you've gone through
There's so much to undo
But I promise you that you can find peace in me
Let me complete the pieces of you that are missing"

Beyond

Our Love is beyond earthly protection
Beyond the logistics of comprehension
Surpassing our controllable action or intention
No need for intervention
For I have overdosed on the cure for my broken heart
I Love you with all of me
Reaching realms of you
I never thought existed
Naturally in depth and in tune with you
Our Love so strong
It stands on its own
Not on the validation of any man
Not for anyone else to understand
Our Love never planned
But naturally conceived
I more than believe in we
So let us be
I need for Love to continue to set us free."

Love's Revelation

What is your conviction?
Let me Love you, no intermission
Nor am I
Intermittently smitten
Consistence
is my gift to you
You never have to mention
All that you've been missin'
Because God revealed that to me too

Unspeakable

Impatiently patient Love
Nothing else that I can think of
Dream of, Breathe in or speak of

With an intimate state of consciousness
So much more than the day before
And every bit of yesterday
I Love you more

Speak freely into my soul
My heart yearns for your approval
This is not something I want to get used to
Keep it new to me
I Love you, what did you do to me?

Thirsty

Quench my thirst
Contribute to my soul
Your knowledge is our power
A standard I must uphold
I will reciprocate
Pour into you as you have into me
Giving you life
To be received abundantly
Eternal fluidity
Powerful entities
Exchange of Love
As your intellect enters me

Afloat

If you see me floating in the universe
Amongst the stars
It's ok, don't come get me
You see
I've found the most beautiful star
And I'm mesmerized by the aura of his brightness
So please, don't get me
Leave me there

Love Comprised

True Love takes sacrifice and compromise
Comprised of truth and diligence
Never to walk away from what may not always be so
evident
Remember why you're here, remember why I care
The root of which we plant our heart and souls
So organic
We grow
Together anything can be attained
Arranged in a supernatural way
Incomprehensible Faith
Never a question of how our
Interconnection is relayed
So certain of what is as what will come to be
So certain of the greatness you possess, but
You act as a mirror to me
That despite the imperfection of my reflection,
You see my beauty

Today's Testimony

I can't imagine what life would be
Without he
And me being swayed
To Love him in the most imperfectly
Perfect way
But today remains a testimony
Of my undying Faith
That God will continue to spare me from
What I thought would keep me imminent
In Love's grace
So I waited
Patiently for what was created for me
I created for he
And we
Have much of forever to remain
Each moment is a glimpse of
What will be
And I cherish what is
To encounter true Love
In this lifetime is truly a privilege

Boundaries

Boundaries were crossed
Your walls came down
My faith surpassed my ego
And Now
You're my personal superhero

Words can't describe how I feel for you
My heart is compelled to Love and care for you
I want to protect and am willing to go
Through it all for you

Interconnected
Energies bound by spirituality
Experiencing things I can't explain
But I am just glad that this is our reality

You're so amazing to me
You give me so much to look forward to
I picture being in your arms
Elated at the thought of being held by you
Love looking in your eyes
They tell me all I need to know

Feeling all of your high's and low's
Even when you're not around
I want you to be happy
And these days, it's all I seem to care about

One touch from you makes me want forever
And I am so grateful for our journey together

Such potent divinity is not guided by timelines

Nor the societal constraints that tends to put strains
On ordinary relationships

We are growing to appease God's morale
instead of our own
Substantial foundation to be rooted in
Sacrifice is true testament of desire for God's Love

And by God's will and grace, you are now my husband

Reminisce

Your sensations surpassed my intellect
My will to control,
Diminished my want to forget
All I could remember,
Was…
You, your aura,
And unspoken memories of our collective energy
When I hugged you
Reminiscent of something I've felt
Yet, something completely new
So nostalgic… so comforting
I felt you;
And I was ever so cognizant
Of what you needed
Though we conceded
My conviction proceeded
And I gave you what God told me you needed;
A concept greater than I could grasp
Fulfilled his will despite my own plans
I would take how I feel for you over a rational explanation any day
Because I find comfort in the ways you show your Love to me

Love Expound

Love found and I expound
Greatness
Fear is seized
Failure is accepted
The known path to greatness will not be redirected nor
neglected
In the name of comfort
A distorted image or control is not the answer
The real answer is to let go
Of all that we've known to be true
Comfort won't allow our souls to grow
In truth
So undo the residue of disappointment
Bask in the anointment
Of his saving grace
Love me, all of me without remorse
Fear not my bodily extremities because they can be used
to Love you more
I am a vessel
Bask in the aroma of my authenticity
Spiritually inclined to give you the best of me
Until the end of me
I am overwhelmed by your aroma
Breathe you in
And be the solution to your solitude
Let me Love you beyond the confines of your ego
Release control and allow for the need to be Loved
And wanted to take over

I will submerge you in the greatest kiss of all time
For a lifetime

Speaking in tongues, a language only you and I can understand
I Love you past our bodily intimacy
Past the moisture of my parted lips
As you enter me
Take me on and Love me deeply
I wanna massage your inner most desires with my deepest intentions
Bless me with your divine intervention
And show me all that I've been missing
Love me

Thank You

From the darkness into the light
You're my sun who shines so bright into my dimmed sky

We both wanted to be Loved
Found each other and can't seem to get enough

I will continue to give until I can't breathe
Inhale you and exhale what used to be

The hurt, the pain and the heartache I've endured
Has paved the way
For your Love to enter my heart to stay

So please don't leave me

So long as you're with me, you don't have to ask for
anything

You're more than the King I've depicted in my dreams

My reality superseded my minds perceived notion of what I
confined you to be

Couldn't fathom the thought of you not being around
I'm glad I don't have to

True Love is endless
It carries no burdens
Extends past our worldly bounds

You're more than what I've wanted
I'm not scared to tell the world

That you're who I need

Actions pick up where words fall short

I thank you for being such a giant
I thank you for Loving me

Everything

Love me for everything I am
Love me for everything I am not

Allow my presence to interrupt your life
While I serve my heart's purpose
And fulfill your hopes and dreams

My Love is not too good to be true
It's just true

So when it's good, enjoy it
Instead of letting your insecurities intervene

Dwell in the place I hold dear
My passion for Love, life and us will forever keep you near

Perfect Love Story

And I vow…

You're so much more than my soul mate
But my twin flame
God placed you on my heart while I was mending my own pain
I obeyed
But I was confused
That somehow, on my personal journey
I was compelled to protect your heart and pray for you
I dreamt you
I saw the kindness in your eyes
I wanted to mend your heart and make you smile
I don't know why but your well being became my priority
I don't know why
But I just wanted you to be ok
And I trusted in God's way
Because I knew he wouldn't lead me astray
I knew we had a purpose for finding each other
Even if it was just my role to restore your trust in Love and faith
Whatever you needed
Somehow my pride conceded and restoration of your ability to Love and trust became what I needed
It was my duty to show you there was hope for true Love and genuine character
It was my duty to show you that I wasn't rattled by your resistance; though you subjected me to your armor
And you wanted me to believe your heart was bulletproof, you wanted me to believe you were smooth but when our energies collided, we were too potent for regularity
I knew what you needed,

So I prayed for you with no remorse
I never thought we'd be here
Little did I think we'd be this close
When you're away, I feel incomplete
I miss you the moment you leave me
I get lost in your kindness and warmth
You always make me feel beautiful and your actions reaffirm that my Love is on the right course
Nothing else matters
You've saturated my soul with your good intentions and Love

And I'm overloaded
With you, I'm unplugged
So much freedom in what we express
But it's not reckless
More than purposeful
Waded in the depths without fear of drowning
You are my crowned King and we have forever to reign.
I Love you

CULTURALLY SKEWED

There's so much pain and disparity all around. Racism has been quiet but in the age of social media, it has plagued and enlightened the likes of everyone. Racism has never died; it's just been made more prevalent through everyone having access to technology. I do believe that some, if not most of it is propaganda to perpetuate a much greater agenda than racism. Essentially, what people don't understand is that it's not about race, gender, culture as much as it is about MONEY. And all of these sub-factors keep us collectively disoriented and unable to unify to fight the bigger problem which are, CORPORATIONS; because that is who has control. We are all disposable; human life is not valued in this country and it is evident in what they monetize.

There is a Human war yet Blacks continue to be the scapegoat after building this entire country and being psychologically and violently oppressed and raped in every way imaginable to man. As much as I would like to pretend it doesn't exist, my race and experience don't allow me to. People in power know how to play on everyone's insecurities to keep their power and money allotted to the wealthy few that run the country and basically the world. I wish people understood that we are all human and bleed the same blood; that hating another will not make you better or make things better for you.

How could you hate someone because of the COLOR of their skin which is how they were BORN; it doesn't even make sense. We've been innately taught to police ourselves, I am afraid of being pulled over by the police because of their excessive counts of violence and misconduct with no repercussion. The disregard for Black life is so blatant it almost makes me feel like there is purpose to it. Like, people can't possibly be that ugly, bigoted, racist or unkind.

What does a Black woman with a Black family and a Black husband who will have a Black baby do? How do you plan a future with your Loved one or go about raising your children in a world like this; explain that they have targets on their back because of the color of their skin. How do they then grow up NOT feeling insecure or unsafe? Survival shouldn't be on my bucket list…

I believe in humanity. But reality believes in disparity. Attempting to find the common ground between human rights, stereotypes and justice

Hue

I will not apologize for my hue
I will not apologize for what you want but cannot undo
My Blackness
My Blackness scares you, so you're up in arms
Striking me down with your systemic injustices and insecurities yet, I still find pride and strength to wear my crown
For it can never be removed
I came from Gods and Goddesses, genius, innovation and strength
And since history's tainted past, your hate is our conviction
You stopped waving your batons and picked up your guns
Shooting and killing us by the hundreds
Not just my brothers but my children, my mom, my sisters and cousins
What is it that you fear so much?
So much hate for yourself, so you propel
Not just black, but a human being
You're a coward no matter how many you kill
You're a loser because of all that you steal
I am representative for all you can't stand
I am the voice for the voiceless

I am Sandra Bland.

Lessons

Their delegation and deliberation do not determine your worth
Hundreds of years of separation and when we unify, they find another way to preserve
Their dominance and validate their feeling of inferiority
Mediocrity is the mindset to stagnate greatness and progression
We marched in the 60's and still standing with our hands up
Surrender
Exactly where they want us to be
Complaining and standing still
Thinking peace will resolve years of brown complected misogyny and emasculinity
As our culture continues to deteriorate
They continue to decapitate
Our men
Role reversal is more than an implication
They've been sterilizing our generation and the ones to come
Pants so low, might as well take em off and put a dress on
Women lost in the culture of vanity instead of preservation of family
Teaching children it's ok to live without daddy
Feminist concepts leading to the destruction of the black home
But how is she supposed to cope when she has resentment because she's all alone?
Society demoralizes and dehumanizes our concepts of what it is to Love and marriage is supposed to be
I wish we'd understand
I wish we'd understand that unity is the key

To salvation
So many degrees of separation, it will be hard to become
one and find a solution
To our demise and regression
When will we learn the lessons?

Black men

Black men
How I adore you
The schematics of society downplay your power
They play into your security
Destroy you openly
And in turn keep you captive with the same laws you abide
to
Misguided through education
Struggling to provide for your family
Thoughts suicidal
So you run these streets
The starvation of truth
To be what they've destined you to be
Or to free your mind enough not to be
Subdued
I King you
They tear you down because of all you can do
The infliction of their insecurities, are systemic
Making you feel like being a Black man is an epidemic
But it is a God given birth right and He runs through your
veins
And it is your God given right to just be and not have to
explain
Your Blackness
For your power far supersedes anything that they could
ever sustain
Took them centuries to try to conquer you
And you still do sh*t your own way
Be aware of your royalty and the true context
Of what your people are and what they endured
Do not let them destroy what you were built for
Do not let them define what you're here for

What Do I Tell Him?

What do I tell my son?
What do I tell him?
How do you raise a Man before he is allowed to be a child?
Why am I scared to procreate in a world where his value isn't seen as worth while
Will my Love be enough to protect him from a gun?
How do I tell him, he is convicted before even standing a trial?
Where does he go when my arms are not enough?
How does he thrive when nothing ever seems good enough?
How do I explain that no matter his choice, someone already chooses?
How do I protect him and not lose him?

Brown Complected

Rejection of brown complexion
Failure to acknowledge your hue
Rejection of brown complexion
What the hell are we supposed to do?
Failure to account for the origin of our history
Lost in translation
So it makes no sense to me
And you…
Have become what they wanted us to be
Fervently unaccountable

Tainted Vision

Perception is reality
But visions are skewed
One party creates the temperament
While the other gets accused
Guilty because of hue
But the reason for hatred is deflection
Controlling us by any means necessary
Blacks cannot be their own disciplinary
Separation has left us compromised
Vulnerable, yet still fail to see our own demise
As monetary factors remain a guise
And seemingly make those with wealth,
"blind"
Thinking they're unaffected
They continue to remain objective
Meanwhile their complexion remains a hard unlearned lesson
You're still you
Your money doesn't validate you
Take that wealth away
Put you on a block or maybe a traffic stop
Maybe that'll change your perspective
Make you more vocal and perceptive
Your dollar won't stop you from being hunted

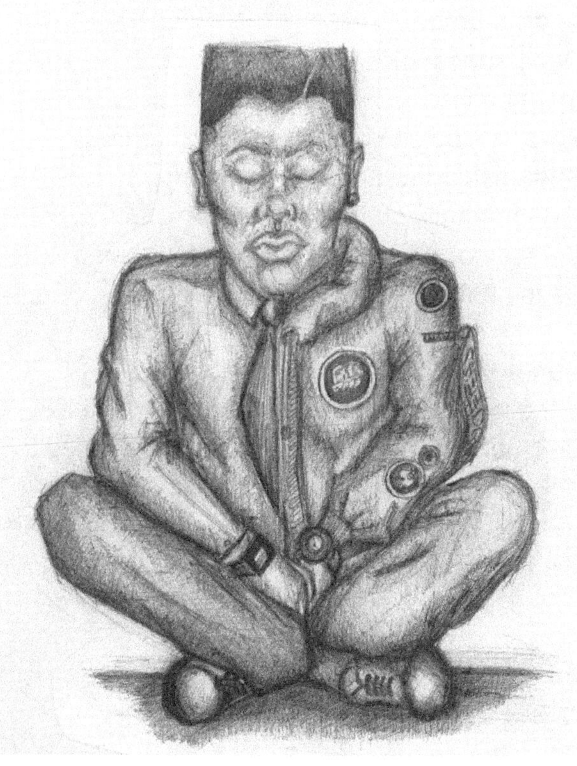

Hey Black Man

Hey!
Black man!!
Pick up your head
Walk with your back straight and chest out
There may be fear in your heart but don't be misled
For there is power ordained by God in each of your steps
There is fight in each heart beat
All the more reason the death of your spirit is their target

Well behaved black man
Don't be discouraged
Get off your knees; pick up your feet
And fight to be free
Pick your pants up so you can walk with pride
Do not hide behind what money can buy
Do not let them tell you that you're free
Do not let their atrocities that plague your being
Continue to contain you psychologically
Hey!!
Black man!!
You are the leader of the past, present and future
Hey Black man, you're who they have to get used to
Hey Black man… do not reside in mediocrity
Do not remain imprisoned in what they set you out to be
You are a King

Still Ain't Listenin'

Inaccurate depictions
Immoral descriptions
Cultural demolition
But black people still not listenin'
Blindly conditioned
Psychologically scripted plays
And we are on stage
Shuckin' and jivin'
We blame and displace
Unity will break the barrier of our jaded
Sentiment and anger
Be conscious, be active and pray
Do not perpetuate the self hate

Impulsive Truth

Implosion or explosion
Expulsion of your truth
Constant demise
While others surmise
That you're angry all the time
But all of what you endure cannot be
Summarized or understood
Dehumanization and misrepresentation of your Blackness
and womanhood
Constant defense
You can never just be
Your own men degrade you
Other cultures mimic your appearance
At the same time they forbade you
Robbing you of your very existence
You are forsaken in the name of feminism
A concept made to keep the Black man out of the home
prevalent
Degradation so evident
Your strength is so relevant; but that energy is misdirected
Technology so prevalent but we can't seem to autocorrect
On a mission to find our collective self respect…

American Dream

The American Dream
I want no parts of it
Because that dream wasn't meant for me to fit
Deception in history books
School starts the basis of our corrupted knowledge
Learning about selective African American figures
So we don't feel too empowered
Hey! Why don't you improv on your morals
So you can get a piece of this American pie
Diabetes laden, color barren slice
That most compromise their lives for just to die
That sh*t wasn't made for you
Who do you think you are?
Think because "they" offered you a slice
You'd be a part of…

Na, just another distraction from the main event
Just like the election of a black President
The lapse of his power is evident
Because our nation is run by corporations

One government under God
Invisible with justice for them
Never for you
So, remember that before you fight for your
Red, white and blue

Whoop, Whoop
Sirens flash
Illegally searching your character
Molesting your dreams
Creating schemes

While you're chasing this nightmare they've
Convinced you to call a dream
Keep chasin' that cream
Keep chasin' that cheddar
Keep convincing yourself
That focusing on this "American Dream"
Will make sh*t better

A Letter to Ms. Coretta

Ms. Coretta
Did you believe your King had a vendetta?
Yes, he impacted the Black community greatly
But could he have Loved you better?

I don't mean to judge
You sticking by him meant you forgave him and didn't hold
a grudge
But did you ever get the nudge
To leave?

I mean no disrespect
But do you feel your Loyalty was inept
For a man not deserving of a Queen?

I'm sorry
I don't mean to be harsh
I know you Loved him with all of your heart

But he should've done better by you
He is honorable to mention
But he should've recollected
In the times that he traveled, what he truly set out to do

His legacy shouldn't have been to allude
To
Infidelity
Part of his Legacy should've been to include
Being Faithful to you

You didn't let his actions change your heart

So, I commend you
For seeing past your personal hurt
I commend you
For knowing the movements worth
I Love you for being the phenomenal woman that you are

I admire you for being our saving grace from the very start

Revolution

There is no evolution without Revolution
There will be war
There must be casualties
But change will erupt
And it is what we need
For your society is being depleted of human beings
In a sense of having compassion for not another
Not physicality

It is in tragedy that we will find peace
Commonality
We are all one

Celebrity Accountability

Celebrity Accountability
You rather play it safe
Hiding behind fame when you're the most insecure of us all
Cameras block our view of your reality
While people idolize your flaws
No matter what you do, it's important
Validation on a constant basis
No wonder your ego is so potent
Smelling like sh*t
Poverty pervades our communities
No social accountability
So many people look to you but you've strayed away from
the path our Civil Rights Leaders set
If it wasn't for them
You wouldn't be on the platform you stand; so why not
take a stance
Instead of corporate compliance and reliance on riches
Poppin' champagne and talking about b*tches
Extend your knowledge to your fans
Speak on what's really important; what's really at hand
Instead you play it safe
Wouldn't want you sponsors to flake
God forbid you step all the way up
And speak all the way out
God forbid you show us how strong you can be
God forbid you live by example
You claim it's not your responsibility to inflict your views or
lifestyles on us
But we pollute our minds every time we buy your albums or
hear your song in the club
You know how powerful it would be if you took some
accountability?

Do you deserve your never ending ego to be fed?
The attention and riches are all you seek
Draining your community's pockets because we buy your CD's
With that dough we spend, you reap your seed
Not even generous to feed starved children in your communities
Starved from food, starved from education
Starved from intellect
Starved from the dignity to live without pondering death.
Not asking you to save the world, but take a stance
Encourage future generations to have more of a chance

Which god Do You Serve?

A god of war
A god of gender
A god of things seen
Not to be confused with the spiritual being in me

Confined by the rules and regulations of what man has
taught
Brainwashed impoverished folk while they continued to
slaughter

Daughters, wives, sons, used husbands to kill
Absent from home, never to teach their son necessary
skills

How to be a man, without a gun but a peaceful plan
How to stand firm in what is right
Not the general consensus and fraud from "our" country's
plight
They are whatever they sell to you, not the truth as what is
really is
Conveying blasphemous phrases onto the most innocent
of ears
Ears desperate to hear hopes of their future that murder
will bring us
False sense of safety from a government for them, by them
controlling us with a mind f*ck

Feels so good, then the climax comes
Left with nothing but white stuff
The potent plan to kill of all colors and cultures of men

Ok then? What god do you serve?

Heavy Load

I can feel the weight of the world on my chest
Every beat of my heart, another life lost
Another gun shot being sawed off into someone's flesh

Life is a gift of which we'll never understand the cost
With a reactive state of mind in this life; all value seems to
keep getting lost
Ego's immersed in narcissism; dipped in impatience with a
sprinkle of ignorance
Ignorance which results in unaccountability
We are blind because we don't want to see
We leave the truth where it stands and chase immediacy
and mediocrity
All because we feed our far gone flesh with worldly woes
But that's why we feel so incomplete
We force feed our spirit to gain external validity
Only God knows the grave we've all dug ourselves
How we blatantly put faith on the shelf
We call His name in vain or in pain
And expect him to come running to our aid to help
Have mercy on us all
The state of humanness is flawed
With a never ending need to feed the right now's
We have to have faith and that entails us not always
knowing the how
But our sense to control leads us astray
Because we curse the day with the same lips that pray
Wonder why the devil is so near
While we clench onto hopelessness and fear
All while we speak of having faith
Never to possess the belief of a better tomorrow

We announce death with our words and wonder why we live a life of sorrow
But this, can change
When we put God first and stop living life our way

Just-Us

In this country, Black lives seem so disposable
While considered culturally deplorable

We fall victim to self hate
Things haven't gotten much better since the slavery days
Instead of standing up for what is right;
We rather stand in line for a pair of J's

We can't expect justice when we won't even vote to elect
officials we can actually trust in
Yet, complain about a system
Set up for our demise
Black people need to rise to the occasion
Our culture needs saving
Stop being segregated by textures of hair and skin tone
Who cares if you're considered "dark skinned" or a "red
bone"

It's about standing in the face of wrong until we get right

So get it right or get left

FINDING ME AND FINDING GOD
THROUGH WOMANHOOD

Women are divine and heavenly beings. We are able to carry life in our bodies and give birth. We are majestic, strong, graceful and powerful. Living in a world where women have learned to objectify themselves and call it feminism and empowerment; living in a world where women are over-sexualized openly, just about EVERYWHERE but are shamed for breastfeeding in public. We are taught to base our confidence on the sexualization of our body parts and learn that we are here to gratify and satisfy others. We are taught that we are less than if we do not fit a societal mold of beauty; a mold that forever changes. We are taught to live a life of insecurity because we are never enough.

My false sense of womanhood and confidence was fed by attention from others. Using what people said to feel good about myself or reject myself. External Validity was my enemy. But, I admit, I hadn't fully grasped what it really entailed being a woman until I experienced my first and only pregnancy, 3 years ago. Sadly, I had a Partial Molar pregnancy and my baby could not survive full term. It was through the complications in my physical body, my emotions, my mind, soul and heart that I felt no one else around me understood. The lonely feeling of being depressed as my body quickly plummeted into post partum; feeling worthless and guilty like I should've done more but I couldn't; that was just the reality. Recovering from that brokenness, I was able to learn how to value and Love myself more. I learned how strong a woman has to be to carry life and how it's so much more than physicality. She has to be strong enough to endure all that comes with the process and truly be selfless; disregarding her own will for the betterment of the unborn. I mean this in physicality and metaphorically.

I learned that being a Woman is Godly just in the simplicity of who we are naturally. Honor your abilities because they are endless. Do not limit yourself to what others expect you to be. Most importantly, you are Divine. Your nurturing nature and innate ability to Love past your own well being, brings Life to the unborn.

Forgiving yourself is pertinent before you begin to understand how to forgive others

Forgive

Forgive because it's the human thing to do
Forgiveness does not alleviate accountability from the others who have wronged you
But gives you a strong foundation to build strength
And compassion of your character
Do not base your good merit on what others are doing or what you think they will do
Hurt people hurt people
Break the cycle of ignorance with self awareness
It starts with you

Yesterday's Tears

I cried tears yesterday
And it washed away the pain
To wake up again
To only feel the same

Relentless thoughts of hopelessness
Carrying adversity with finesse
Those approaching me would never
Know of my own demise
Why I have these dark circles under my eyes
That I encounter night after sleepless night
Met with dreams of regret
Met with realities I want to forget
Wanting to undo that last sketch
Erase it and start over again

But imperfection is our greatest masterpiece
Accidentally and overtly
Blinded by the disguise of what everyone wants me to be
Intently condemning me to their imagery
Of societal construct and appropriation

Succumbing to the will of others is damnation
While not knowing if succumbing to the will of religion
Will save you from….
What? Who? The why's and how's?
Confining our soul to abuse your source of infinite power
You are worth more than momentary gratification

Greater Than

Sometimes I second and third guess
But that can't be relevant on the quest to greatness
The only way for success to manifest
Is to step out on faith
Despite my feeling of imperfection and inadequacy
Sometimes, I get mad at me
Knowing I'm bigger and better than my fear
That God instilled in me His purpose
And it is my duty to fulfill that
While I'm here…inflection

Exemplary

She exemplifies individuality
While so many exude similarities
Never does she carry
The expectations others have of her
Because perceptions vary
Depending on the set of eyes you choose to see through
Are you a victim or a hero?
Are you a "why me?" or a conqueror
Swallow your pride and ego
Live the life God promised you
Love and humility are fertilizer for your soul
God will forever acknowledge your diligence which
Supersede your immediate gratifications
So, be strong

Clarity

No filter
Transparent
Apparently lucid
Respected, introspective
Worry is so useless
There is power in Love
There is power in kindness
There is power in walking upright
And being righteous
Infinite God; infinite blessings
You deserve it, so just
Believe
Be who God is preparing you to be
Your belief alone, will set you free

Hail

Hail Queen
Full of Grace
Never to feel disgraced in the name of societies
Double standard
Embrace your strength, no regrets
Beget all that has been intentionally portrayed and never forgotten
Like men treating your womb as their controllable option
The power lies in how you see and carry yourself
What would Ma'at do?
God-like, giver of life
No wonder men have strived to subdue you,
Queen
Beauty seen, true power subdued
Don't let them tell you what you can or can't do
Give all you can, don't worry about what's received
Or by who
You are given the right tools to unveil truth
Black goddess, you were chosen before you decided to choose

Quest for Truth

On a quest for truth
Religion has been used as a noose
For hopes of better
But we choke to death
While we remain complacent
Without challenging
Without acknowledging
That they have stolen our spirits and ideologies and
They lack originality
Pieces of our own history segmented, for our demise
Willingly submitting to a lobotomy
Bottom feeders; validation seekers
Awaiting the change they'll never willingly give up
Jesus where are you? What do we do?
I'm on an intuitive quest for the Black Christ
Because I need to identify
Glory be to the most high, we are innately designed and
inclined
Just have an open heart and mind
The truth exists where intuition and passion collide

She's Enough

She approaches the day
With remnants of yesterday on her breath
Talking about what she could've done
On her endless list of accomplishments
Procrastination plagues her actions
Insecure thoughts give her doubt
Pursuing her dreams with action
Seem like such a dangerous route
But conformity is no longer acceptable

Due Date

I tried to make sense of it
I tried to connect with it
The greater purpose that is
A very painful truth
There is nothing I can do
To bring you back
There are times I wonder how much more I could've Loved
you
I wonder how much better I would be with you in my life
Am I selfish for wanting you here?
But your presence just wasn't in the final plans
You were the hardest lesson; my biggest heartbreak
I lost you, I lost a piece of me, but gained so much
appreciation for what could've been because of how much
better your loss has made me
Your life was not in vain; though I am still mending the pain
I learned to Love life in such a different way

07-17-2013

Life is a Gift

Life is a gift
And we wait until the tomorrow's to unwrap
Each moment should be lived
And we must realize that
The real present is in our present
So do not bask in what has not yet come to fruition
Real time requires our presence
Decisions require our intuition

Wombman

Wombman
You've birthed many
While takers of life, drain you plenty
In their attempts to subdue you
Within the constructs of society
Your will, never to be shattered by any

Black Wombman

With your protruding hips, thick lips glorious hair in all your
goodness
I Love you
Do you Love you?
You should
The inferiority they feel around your grace, is not to be
misunderstood
Recognize your divinity
You're innate actualization of strength as you muddle
through the remnants of our lost Black men
White washed tendencies, mending your heart and
mending his so you can tend to Communities, so as to
restore our brokenness
Do not forget who you are
Embrace the tears Fight through it all, until you have
nothing left to give
But first, remember to restore your truth
You are the beginning of nations
Your hue consists of Godly magnitude
Black woman, I Love you
Do you Love you?
External validation is meant to subdue you
Break free your chains of momentary gratification,
expectation and be the Love you so desire
We are built to give but it is never more than we can bare
You are the way and the light, illuminate the way you know
is designed to be right

Love Lost

Let me give you what I didn't have
So my heart can mend the lack of Love I so desperately
needed
So that when I give unto you, your expectations will be
superceded
You won't have to ask me
I'll just be there
You won't have to do without or question if I care
Your needs will come before mine and I'll always have time
Let me Love you beyond the confines of motherhood, past
the times you can't stand me and feel misunderstood
I will never forsake or break your heart
You will be a big part of the reason I live
Future child of mine, I have so much Love to give

Right to Be

Forgive yourself
Life's adversities make it hard to be perfect
You don't have to be perfect but just know that you're worth it
Worth more than your eyes can see, hands can touch and mouth can say
It's an internal knowing
Collective intuition including all of your senses
But
We have imaginary standards in which we force ourselves to fit
And that's not ok
We can't move forward until we feel like we've paid
And that may be our way of punishing ourselves with self inflicted pain
Staying in relationships we don't deserve
Recounting negative actions and experiences until they're heard by the universe and Given permission to be
There's only one you and me
We are taught to pass forgiveness on to others
Never granting ourselves the right to be free

Lord, Remember Me

Genetic predisposition omits remission of insane tendencies
Leniency, please remember me
As I say this prayer
Asking God to peel back these layers
Until my core is reached
Restore me, fill me with destiny
A future beyond my past pain
I need help removing my worth from this disdain I have for my name
I thought I surpassed the limits of my could have beens
But I over-think and create should have beens before I even got to them
Feel this raw truth
Isolation from the masses
Forgiving others; quickly letting them re-enter my virtue
Tainting my will, I victimize myself throwing myself in demise
There is no surprise that the closest to me are disguised
With nothing but what they can gain from me, in mind
So now, it's time to let go of this hell I created
So I await Heaven's elation hoping my soul hasn't been too degraded

Left Wondering

Faced with opposition
In constant search of resolution
Amidst confusion
I try to stay rooted in divine truth
But I may be fooled
And find my ways engulfed in shallow intentions and
momentary gain
Human variation of societal corrode
Flesh infested actions
Wondering why I can't reach the greatness desired

Cover Up

I am Flawed
In awe of the daily preparation to validate my extremities
Instead of taking the time to replenish me on the inside
What no one else can see
Disguising my flaws so that I will not be harshly judged
Acting like I don't care
But I absolutely give a f***
I convince myself and say, well at least I don't wear much make-up
But with each application there is so much I am trying to cover up
I can distract the world but I cannot hide from me
Because in my own reflection I do not always like what I see
Clarity is what I seek yet I walk out everyday in disguise
Hypocritical in my views of just being myself

Magnify

She magnifies and glorifies God even as she wept
The delivery of her message will come at any expense
The price she was willing pay to pave the way for
generations of women
To proceed would be more than she could ever profit
Walk in grace but be ready to fight
Do not let a man determine your worth
God made you in Love and that is what you so deserve
Keep walking even when you don't' know your way
Be all that you are
Get rid of what you think you aren't or can't do
You cannot prove what you have not attempted to do
Do not live in fear!

Only Way

I Love how society crushes our power and potential
Overly concerned with underpaid jobs and rent being due
We are all subdued in the confines of debt
Waste of energy climbing a never ending ladder to attain
glory
And what do we glorify?
Monetary valued THINGS
They can be replaced
But we often deny our soul and entire entities of freedom
How?
By obsessing, possessing and engulfed in our ego
We are driven by pride; neglecting our hearts which are
destined to live in Love
The root of it all
Bask in humanity
Engulf your energy in purpose
Fulfill the deepest desires of your heart
The truths of your soul
It is the only way

SOCIAL MEDIA CHRONICLES

We live in a society plagued with immediate gratification. The more technology and social media sites there are, the more people race to do the most outlandish things for attention. From women getting naked, people videotaping obscene acts; all for likes or to trend and psychologically, to feel like we're relevant.

Seems like we live in a warped reality where everyone is obsessed with a false sense of confidence that comes from how much other people validate perceived realities. Social media, for some, is a way to portray a different person than the reality of who they are. Either way, people have lost touch of what it is to just be... Not so much concerned with the genuineness of the attention they receive but it's just about attaining more than the next person.

How much do you compromise for likes?

IG vs. ID

Contrast so vast
And
Focused on Hue
Filters alter complexions
Altering flawed visions of you
Flaw is perceptual
Imagery distorted to individual perfection
Denial of true self
Ego misdirected
Unaffected
Neglected
What is your truth?
What does your filter undo?

Propaganda vs. Truth

There is a war going on
Propaganda vs. truth
Accuracy vs. social media
And neither uncouth
Over-saturation can be debated
But we are highly impacted by the negativity that is infiltrated
Current events on a whim, with the click of a button
Proactive and worried minds lose focus in the moment
Reacting with actions of enforcement but nothing that will sustain
Our idea of protesting is taking a stance on Facebook to complain
Assassination of our attention span, before we can process one ideal
We get hit with some more information
What do you do?
How do you decide?
Where is the medium where reality and media collide?
What is truth when our own perception alters the depth of our realities?
How do we integrate reality into social media's anatomy?

Skewed Vision

Altering your body because your vision is skewed
It seems that no adjustment is ever good enough
And nothing is satisfying to you
Emotional and psychological baggage displaced into vanity
Thinking if we fix our exterior that we would be happy
Society has always been a culprit in the breakdown of our
spirit
Social media, much like cocaine to a drug addict; makes
us think that everything can change with just that one hit
That the changes we need to make are IG filters after
taking selfies with
Our selfie sticks
How narcissistic can we get?
Imaginary haters being addressed
You like the attention; whether bad or good
Claiming to be philosophical and misunderstood
But you're just a fraud
Or maybe you're just afraid
Of what people might actually say
If you're just you
What do you look like behind the mask you wear?
The one that everyone sees you in, clicks like but really
doesn't care

Plagiarism

Everyone doesn't need a platform
Social media provides just that
Everyone doesn't need a platform
Not everyone uses discretion or uses tact
Social media; where people use filters to disguise their true identities
Where word play is plagiarism staged as original thought and philosophy

Perpetratin' for Admiration

People want to be admired
So they post they flick up
Filters changing their appearance;
More than just caked up make-up
Hiding the truth to their identity;
Fools gold
Wrapped in deceit awaiting validation
Because their confidence lies in the lies
That Instagram holds
Pose ma' flick it up
Maybe you might find a man to light ya wrist up
Infamous status, showing off nothing that matters
You cherish what he has
So he gonna cherish what you post,
That ass

Loaded ASSets

Many women wanna carry the load
But don't know how it really go
We're taught that our ASSets are a burden
We don't get to choose
But YOU get to go to a surgeon
And society accepts you as beautiful
Then we compete and overexpose
Not understanding the true value is more than what's
under our clothes
Fighting for the spotlight
Women, before you fought for the right to be dignified
And freedom came with a price
Now, women get naked and buss it open for a share and a
100 likes

For the Gram

Do it for the gram hoe
Do it for the gram hoe
But don't bet ya life
There is way too much competition
When you live your life for the likes
Too many lips, hips and fake tits
You trip and grip on over-sexualized comments and mentions
How are you such a bad b*tch but can't live without that attention?
There are so many like you
Be original
Your ass being fatter doesn't mean you're one of a kind
It means you many keep his attention for 10 seconds instead of 9
So, do it for the gram hoe
I'm not hatin'
I'm just tryna understand though
Why settle for being a bad b*tch when being a Goddess is what you were designed for?
Mother of all things created, know your power
Love yourselves past visual and oral fixations
Stop selling your soul for seconds of admiration

Baring your soul is no easy task but when you're an artist, you know that the plan is much bigger than you hiding your personal struggles. You are compelled to share your pain in hopes of giving another permission to find their freedom through exposure and honesty. Exposure is empowering and it is what we chose to expose that will be given life. Attention seekers often abuse this privilege.

Art is give and take, with a lot more give.

It's not about the money or attention for SOME of us...it's truly about the ability to inspire others.

Iesha

Iesha hails from New York and graduated from Sacred Heart University with a Bachelor of Science in Criminal Justice. Iesha is a God fearing woman who's relied on her Faith to push through adversity in her life as well as finding the strength to persevere. Iesha, just married in November 2015, with the support and encouragement of her husband, has decided to quit her job to pursue her dream of becoming an accomplished author. With this being her first book, she is currently working on her second, has already sketched out ideas for her third and will also delve into writing Children's books. She also plans on creating a service providing personalized poetry for special occasions as well as personalized greeting cards. There is no limit to this journey and Iesha is ready to take on all that this debut has to offer! You can also find her on social media!

Facebook: Iesha Williams

Wordpress: Rebelutionary85.wordpress.com

Twitter: @Rebelutionary85

IG: beautifulcontradiction